ILLUMINATION

Spiritual Emergence and the Evolution of the Soul

Carrieanne Fonger

BALBOA.
PRESS

A DIVISION OF HAY HOUSE

Fonger, Carrieanne, 1971-
Illumination : spiritual emergence and the evolution
of the soul / Carrieanne Fonger.

1. Self-actualization (Psychology). 2. Self. I. Title.
BF637.S4F63 2012 158.1 C2012-902840-1
Golden Sun Books
www.carrieannefonger.com
1st Printing 2012
Printed in Canada
Editing and Design by 4th Floor Press, Inc.
www.4thfloorpress.com

Balboa Press books may be ordered through booksellers or by contacting:
Balboa Press
A Division of Hay House
1663 Liberty Drive
Bloomington, IN 47403
www.balboapress.com
1-(877) 407-4847

Printed in the United States of America
ISBN: 978-1-4525-6799-0 (sc)
ISBN: 978-1-4525-6800-3 (e)
Balboa Press rev. date: 02/07/2013

For all the brilliant souls who have courage to light the way.

ILLUMINATION

Spiritual Emergence and the Evolution of the Soul

table of contents

introduction

The real voyage of discovery consists not in seeking new lands, but seeing with new eyes.

Marcel Proust (1871 – 1922)

My childhood was spent playing with angels. Ever present like family, they have always been at my side. Seeing these glowing beings in spirit form was a magical way to learn about the world. We shared many exciting adventures together as they taught me about spirit: understanding its aliveness, its energy, and its character.

In our shared silence they explained that I was also spirit and my purpose in life was to help others. At four years old, I did not question. My mother knew about my imaginary angel friends, and I told her point blank what they had said. She nodded with a big grin, a twinkle in her eye, and replied, "That must be a wonderful thing for you to know."

This information was not a surprise to my mother. By this time she had already spent many years researching the mysteries of metaphysics and learning how to see energy and angels. She taught me a form of hands-on-healing, and together we would play with energy and test our knowledge of the unseen. My entire childhood was spent living in the world of spirit. It became my language of being, framing a reference for all things.

This unique perspective of life endowed me with the magical spirit of a young child, right into my adolescent years. However, as each year passed, I drew deeper into a place of high school, friends, and work that came to be known as the "real world." Full of jealousy and greed and squashing down others to get ahead, this world was completely opposite to the kind and gentle place of spirit that I grew up in. In an effort to survive, I began to create a new Carrieanne, one that would mould and shape into what everyone in the real world considered 'normal.' I forgot about the angels and their lessons in spirit and its aliveness within all things, especially within myself. I forgot about who I was and what I was here to do. From time to time, my mother would ask if I could still see the angels and would remind me of my childhood with them, but it was lost on the deaf ears of an adolescent trying to make my way in the world.

It was a very sad time for me, drifting through life, trying to make the best of the chaotic mess I had created for myself as someone else. Then something unexpected happened: my mother was diagnosed with cancer and within eight months died from the disease. My whole world turned upside down in a flash, forcing me to ask questions about myself: Who am I? What is important to me? Why am I here?

I didn't have the answers. I couldn't remember. The loss forced me to go within and search spiritually. The endless questioning made me remember my childhood and who I was at the core: a spiritual being. One by one, I shed the protective masks and moved gently into rediscovery of myself in the language of spirit. The resulting transformation that I endured over a period of nine years ripped me apart and tore me to shreds. It stripped me right down to the core and then slowly, carefully, put me back together again. I have come to call this pattern of destructive chaos and restoration "the evolution of the soul."

Imagine my surprise, when years later, as a feng shui consultant and teacher, I was helping people go through the same journey! I was encountering people from all walks of life who were going through the same pattern: a traumatic event triggering a spiritual emergence, followed by the evolutionary soul growth process that I had completed just a few years earlier. It was remarkably revealing.

It has been such a gift to work with people to overcome different stages in this process of transformation, allowing me to clearly mark out and define a series of steps that the soul takes on its journey into higher awareness. What's even more important is having gone through the experience myself, I can demystify and simplify the evolutionary changes that you are going through now.

This book is a detailed guide intended to direct you

on your pilgrimage of self-discovery as your soul evolves into higher awareness - a process of transforming the darkness within into the energies of light and love. The mission begins with the self and a focus on "*I am*," leading to a greater understanding of "*We are*." As your soul engages in the creative process of making connection to spirit by releasing the dark and heavy aspects of the ego, you will come to realize that there is more within you than you ever knew before.

During the journey, the trials and tribulations of each of your life tests will reveal your personal belief systems. At each new level of your awareness, new belief systems will form, while old ones will fall away. The resulting expanding awareness will move you into a new understanding of yourself, your world, and your role in it, ultimately allowing you to remember your divine self.

What is your heart telling you? In a time filled with anguish and despair, truth and certainty call out to all souls, begging each individual to awaken to his or her true self. Everyone hears the call, but many ignore it. You have chosen this book because you have heard the call. You feel an overwhelming emptiness and intense restlessness, stirring deep within your soul. The jobs and environments that once supported you become foreign and bland, and the ordinary world exposes its true nature as a world without soul. You feel lost, dazed and confused, unaware of why you are here or if your life has any meaning.

From the moment of that stark realization, you begin the search. Something within begs you to move on, to dig deeper into life, and rediscover something that you long for every day but don't have the words to describe. As you begin to recognize synchronicity and coincidence tapping you on the shoulder, life takes on a more mystical quality, revealing a secret: physical reality is an illusion. Beneath the façade of the ordinary world lies another one hidden, one in which everything is alive and breathing with its own personality and character. A world full of riches and potentials beyond your wildest imaginings awaits, where your divine self can explore the sacred world of the soul.

All that is required for the sacred to appear is to regain the resplendent wonder and reverence for life and your place in it. This magical part of your world is an intrinsic part of your soul and the essence of who you are. Rediscovering the sacred is a revealing journey. It doesn't focus on the outside world of physical surroundings or on the inside world of the mind. The sacred is a delicate meeting of the two worlds, both the inner and the outer, blending them together, seeking to understand how one cannot exist without the other.

The world is deliberately one of duality. Above exists so there can be a below, the dark of night balances the light of day, and the deep nothingness of black reveals the brightness and purity of white. These are the great opposites that ebb and flow amongst the silent, sacred rhythms of nature. Every living thing upon this planet learns from such duality. Who would know love without hate, happiness without sorrow, or safety without fear? To understand the balance between the external and internal is to understand that the macrocosm of the outer world is merely a reflection of the microcosm that you are in the world.

Awakening to the sacred stretches personal reality so

far that it shatters the fetters of the logical mind. This is an integral part of an ongoing process that refines the ordinary and allows the mystical world of the sacred to shine through. You must eradicate that box labeled "what you know" and look at the world with new eyes. In order to see a new perspective, you must admit that you don't know all the answers. Trust in life to show you how to stretch new muscles. To stretch is to grow, to grow is to change, and to change is to learn. Once you dare to look at the magical and mystical world of soul around you, places that the ordinary does not have access to begin to reveal themselves, permitting sight beyond the illusion.

No journey would be complete without the trials that bring great change, yet most people live in such a world of fear that seeking change is becoming a lost art. You are living in a time when threat to personal safety is a daily concern. The result is that you become dependent on personal comfort zones and safe places because you long to return things to how they were when you felt safe. Too much time is spent seeking to maintain a stasis of your own liking, all the while avoiding the truth that everything must change. Change is the only constant in the universe. Learning to embrace change and its gifts will bring the soul to life and make it grow. A plant that has outgrown its pot knows that it must adapt in order to grow. It will push past its boundaries and shoot its roots right out of the pot. It will alter its usual growth pattern and conserve the sunlight and water that sustains it. A plant knows that if it cannot grow, eventually it will die. And so you are reflected. It is a slow death for anyone who fears change and struggles to stay the same in an ever-changing world.

Change is a curious gift. It's always nipping at your heels, turning the future into the present. Often change is viewed as a rabid dog, its teeth clamped painfully into your delicate skin, usually right about the area of the Achilles heel, where you are most vulnerable. However, for all the bad rap it receives, change should be seen as your ally, not your enemy. You can surf the tide of change or its strong current can pull you under. It is always your choice. And in the making of that choice, you begin the journey into self-discovery.

The word discovery conjures up extravagant images of

finding something that has been lost for ages, revealing hidden treasures of knowledge. Whenever you commit to a path of discovery, you are committing to the same fate. Each time you go on a journey in life, you learn about yourself. It doesn't matter what form the path takes. Whether you are traveling, in a relationship, changing careers, having children, or suffering from an illness, fundamentally all experiences are agents of change. For the neophyte discoverer, this is where the road becomes blocked. It is not just the physical boundaries that need to be conquered, but also the great barrier of fear that keeps the road impassible. Early explorers used the term *ne plus ultra,* or "go no further," on their maps to designate a place that you dare not go beyond. This is exactly where you need to be. You must ignore the zone of safety and push on. Any true explorer knows that fear is an illusion and failing to discover what you seek is a worse fate than the fear of it.

Those countless discoverers throughout history helped to create science as a new branch of knowledge. Through their brave attempts, they proved that there is nothing to fear when time is taken to understand how and why things are. Science represents a radically different and powerful way of interpreting the world. Through intense observation, science organizes and measures nature in a logical way. By focusing on small parts of the big picture, scientists can acquire understanding of the world a bit at a time. However, as more intricate clues to the small picture unfold, the bigger picture disappears. The rhythms, cycles, and patterns of the surrounding environment become forgotten. Science has many answers, but it does not have them all. For all its attempts to understand the world, science still cannot grasp the mysterious.

Science as a field of endeavor looks to the outside world for answers, when the truth is that all of the answers you seek can be found within yourself at any time. In the classic movie *The Wizard Of Oz*, Dorothy endures many trials on her trek to the Emerald City to see the Wizard, only to find that the most powerful man in Oz does not know how to send her home. To her surprise, the Good Witch of the North reveals that the key to going home was always with Dorothy in her ruby slippers. She was unaware that she had the power to do what she wanted the entire time. However, if she had known that she would not have gone on the journey, would she? She would not have met Cowardly Lion, Tin Man, or Scarecrow. She would not have realized her strengths, her heart, and her courage. In essence, Dorothy would not have discovered herself.

"Know Thyself" is a very old phrase, coined by the Greek God Apollo and etched in stone over the entrance of his Oracle at Delphi. When you come to this world, you come to learn about yourself. What brings you great joy? How can you serve? What is your purpose? Knowing these key things is the most fundamental part of being alive. The truth is that until you can answer these questions with confidence, you are not alive. Most of you are born not knowing the answers but will learn them from the world around you through life lessons. Once you understand who you are, and honor your extraordinary gifts, the world becomes a different place. You develop new eyes to see the sacred within, which reveals the sacred that surrounds you.

I believe that the coming years will focus on

discovering the world of the true self within. Each individual has a divine purpose in this world. When you discover your differences as assets, they become keys to understanding how you can serve others and work together for the better of humanity. Discovering your true self is your purpose. It takes hard work and perseverance, but once you are able to see that sacred light, like Dorothy, you will understand that you had the magic within you the whole time.

You are amidst a revolution in consciousness. Humanity is waking up from a deep slumber. It is time to remember your divine potential, claim your divine inheritance, and embrace your awakening heart.

Book One:

Spiritual Emergence

in the beginning

The beginning is the most important part of the work.

Plato

Before the beginning of form and time, there was a void: a dark empty nothingness that served as a backdrop for creation. During this brief period, the only thing in existence was consciousness, which split into two different aspects: that of dark and light. The resulting separation affected all things within consciousness, including you and me.

Scientists explain this moment of singularity that is

thought to have birthed our universe, as the "Big Bang Theory,"[1] a primordial explosion that propelled creation into expansion. Spreading ever further away from its origins, every particle that was once connected continually grows outward into an infinite space-time loop representing a vast cosmic cycle that is eventually expected to return to its source.

Noted psychic Edgar Cayce explains the Big Bang Theory of the creation of the universe as a time when "God exploded into souls,"[2] with each soul possessing a copy of consciousness from its creator, including its origins. Through experiencing the trials and tribulations of the opposites, a soul advances. It learns, grows, makes mistakes, and understands in order to allow consciousness to transform to higher levels of awareness beyond opposites. The purpose of the soul is to evolve through the experience of separation, find its way back to the light of its source, escape duality and become one.

According to Cayce, in the beginning all souls were

---

1 James Gardner. *The Intelligent Universe.* (New Page Books, 2007). p.171-186.

2 Henry Reed. *Awakening Your Psychic Powers.* (St. Martin's Press, 1988). p.138.

given free will as well as all the attributes of God, including imagination, creation, and manifestation. Through patterns created in the imagination, souls projected their psychic God-force into material forms, primarily for the purpose of play. This is remembered in Greek Mythology as the Golden Age of man, an age in which humans were divine, there was no suffering, and all physical pleasures could be experienced. The Mayans also measured time by the ages of man and have a similar understanding of this first cycle as a Golden Age, which they call Galactic Morning, when the solar system is just coming out of the darkness and entering the light of the Central Sun.

The second cycle is referred to as Mid-day by the Mayans, a time when the souls became more evolved, paid more attention to the physical level of vibration, and awareness of the spiritual gradually dimmed. This progressed to the point where the souls forgot the true origins of who they were, where they came from, and what their purpose was. Known biblically as the *fall from grace*, this descent into darkness and ignorance occurred at the same time the Silver Race of man was upon the Earth.

This race suffered from acts of pride because of their refusal to honor one another and to honor the Gods.

The fall of man from grace occurred when divine man developed ego-centered consciousness and fell into a dualistic state, experiencing the notion of "I am" for the first time. Descent of the spirit into darkness, a tendency towards greater materiality and differentiation, brings separation. By descending into progressively denser matter, the soul experiences an increasing detachment and loss of contact with higher spheres of awareness. Increased sense of self and I are reinforced by the needs to satisfy the requirements of the physical body, where food, shelter, and protection from the elements are vital for survival.

Increased density into physical matter, ego-centeredness, and bodily demands enhances conflict between ego and unity, between self and the flow of creation. The ego's concentration on self-motivation and self-interest lead inevitably to competition and conflict, as each ego-individual tries to profit from and get the better of others.

Self-centered concentration on developing individually

at the expense of others causes the soul to fall even further away from its source. Through negative deeds and thoughts, manifesting in various forms of oppression, murder, torture, and perversion, these souls, when they exit the Earth plane, find themselves enmeshed in the denser, lower astral worlds that take on the form of a self-induced personal hell. Even these rebellious souls will learn from their experience of evil. Eventually they will tire of competitive conflict and start looking for a better way to handle the problem.

The Mayan's third cycle progresses to Afternoon, equating with Bronze Age man. This period of time draws less and less light as the solar system begins its descent into darkness, each age slowly progressing spiritually into a darker place than the one previous as the Earth falls farther away from the Central Sun. The men of the Bronze Age used war as a purpose and passion, and were eventually undone by their own violence.

The Mayan's fourth cycle called Late-Night is synonymous with the Heroic Age, when the solar system has entered its farthest reach from the light of the Central

Sun and is essentially plunged into the heart of darkness. During this time the purpose of existence is to suffer from the ravages of war, labor, and daily toil in higher increments until man turns against man and destroys himself in the fifth and last cycle, called the Night Before the Dawn, or the Iron Age, where man continues today.

According to both Mayan and Greek mythology, this cycle continues over and over again in a continuous circle of creation and destruction. Once man destroys himself in the throes of war at the end of the Iron Age, a resetting pattern commences. The world begins again, starting with the Golden Age, moving down the reoccurring cycle through the ages. However, after keeping meticulous records of the dates for each successive age for over 5000 years, the Mayans are famous for ending their tally with December 21, 2012. A specific ending to this cyclic pattern is not an accident. It is a sign of something different on the horizon.

In our present Iron Age, war is the theme. Filled with insatiable, self-motivated aggression and self-interest, man will continue to repeat this course until he consciously evolves to understand that such thinking exercised at the expense of others is ineffectual, ending only in annihilation. Wars and conflicts between nations, ethnic and religious groups, political parties, families and individuals will eventually come to an end when the "I" thinking of war shifts into the peace and loving of "We."

In the growth of this realization, be it individually or collectively, humans at last are coming to the end of the long downward arc of evolution, the phase of competitive individuality. This transitional Night Before the Dawn or the end of the Iron Age, is a critical turning point of balance, where the downward movement into separation away from the creator turns up towards unity with all other life forms. Even with the continual challenges of self versus unity and matter versus spirit, the advantages of collaboration and cooperation, of mutual respect and assistance, will become ever clear. Mankind will yearn to make a shift in consciousness away from the perception of self as an individual, self-contained unit, responsible only to the self and advance into that of one collective soul. As a result, humanity is becoming one connected group with conscious awareness of moving in the same positive direction for all.

Instead of this age ending in destruction and chaos, wiping mankind from the face of the Earth (as history has shown to be the pattern of the past), the potential exists to transcend all suffering in full awareness in this lifetime. Because man has repeated this cycle many times before, the collective memory of the outcome is buried deep within the subconscious mind of the human race. Every living being knows that the only result to this pattern is self-destruction. As each person becomes aware spiritually, this truth will be clear.

The Mayan Calendar measures recurrent creations and destructions of the world.[3] It stops taking count at this time because it marks the end in the cycle of destruction, the end of the age of darkness. This time man will not destroy himself. As man becomes aware, he will evolve beyond it.

---

3 Graham Hancock. *Fingerprints of the Gods.* (Doubleday Canada Ltd., 1995).

the age of enlightenment

In the middle of everything is the sun.

Nicolaus Copernicus

Nicolaus Copernicus was born in Poland in 1473, a time when the Roman Catholic Church ruled all of Europe, dictating not only laws, but also belief systems through orthodoxy. People believed that the Earth was the centre of the universe because the Church said so. Nobody argued the fact.

As an astronomer, Copernicus learned that this was not so. His days spent with the stars revealed the seemingly impossible: a new cosmology suggesting the Sun is at the centre of the universe.

Copernicus knew that any theory contrary to what the Roman Catholic Church claimed would be blasphemous and decided not to print his findings for fear of repercussions. Only after years of urging from friends did Copernicus reluctantly print his theories. The first copy of his book, *De Revolutionibus,* was handed to him on his deathbed in 1543. Everything was as it should be. Copernicus's book was the first small step needed to put a series of life-changing events into motion.

Galileo Galilei, born in 1564, became a renowned astrologer in his day, at a time when Copernicus's discovery was challenging the scientific view of a geocentric universe. Galileo agreed with Copernicus's view of the universe, and in 1616 he went to Rome to persuade the Roman Catholic Church to accept the Copernican theory of a heliocentric universe. Cardinal Bellarmine instructed Galileo to leave it alone, but Galileo felt that the information was too important to ignore. He published his own work on the subject, *Dialogue Concerning the Two Chief World Systems,* which led to his house arrest, where he remained for the rest of his life.

But all was not lost. The small steps that were set into motion by these two men started a revolution in thinking. The word revolution derives from *revolutio* in Latin, meaning "a turn around." As the whispers and gossiping tales of the Sun at the center of the universe spread amongst the people of Europe, the Roman Catholic Church could not ignore its claims any longer. The number of people questioning this new theory brought the subject to a head.

The Catholic Church later accepted the Heliocentric Theory in 1757, allowing man for the first time to think about his spirituality beyond the Church. The discovery of the Sun as the center of the outer world also opened the doors to a new realm of inner discovery. This brave new idea brought on new ways of thinking to the masses, beginning a revolution in consciousness.

Two hundred and fifty years later, the ripples from that revolution are still having an effect. This time it's about the Sun that shines within the heart of man, the inner light from within. A growing awareness of self forces man to ask: Who am I? What makes me unique? How can I make a difference? The changing view from exploration of the world outside of the self to inside of the self shifts the role of the ego. Ego as an exploration of the outer world asks, "What's in it for me?" Ego from the inner world asks, "How can I better myself so that I may be a better person for others?"

Once the process of awakening into awareness has begun, the realization of personal suffering comes to the forefront. The personal questions that are continually being asked of self to overcome suffering cannot be answered truthfully because of the self-protective mechanisms of the ego. Ego will always make excuses to the self to allow the negative results of actions to seem okay and logical. However, this is not the truth. And as the soul yearns to become aware of itself and true to itself, lies will no longer suffice. The search to know becomes the precipice upon which the entire world teeters to and fro, between the comfort of the uncomfortable life you know and the courageous leap of faith into an authentic life. And change

Illumination

cannot come unless you face the truth about yourself, recognize your suffering, and prepare to transcend it.

Although you see what you need to do, you might hesitate to jump into a new way of being. Not sure which way to go? No problem. Life is going to help by giving you a little push.

spiritual emergence

Not all those who wander are lost.

J.R.R. Tolkien

Consciously or not, you are undergoing a process of awakening known as spiritual emergence. Most awakenings are a result of some sort of traumatic crisis in life. It may have been the loss of a loved one, a divorce, a business collapse, a near-death experience, a spiritual revelation, a car accident, or a natural disaster. It could be a terminal illness, loss of a job, intense physical or emotional distress. There are an infinite number of ways to shock the human system into awakening. Going through this process pulls you away from the outer physical world and challenges you to move deeper within. Review of what is important becomes the focus. Who am I? Where do I fit in? Challenging questions about the self prepare you for development into awakening.

These life-altering events activate the spiritual potential within and initiate the unfolding and expansion of your way of being. The shock from experiencing the event of awakening rapidly surges your transformation process forward. It will be intensely disrupting and out of context with your current life, forcing you to put all things on hold and focus entirely on your crisis as you work to survive it.

The old familiar world that no longer supports you is crumbling and falling away to push you through the darkness necessary to provoke the spirit into waking. Spiritual emergence is a natural process. There are no pills to take, no quick fixes. Good thing. As you explore yourself throughout the duration of this process, you will discover that there is nothing wrong with you. You don't need to be fixed. Instead, what is required is a nurturing of your self, care of the soul within, and tending to the body, mind, and spirit as a whole.

The purpose of your life is to discover who you are. The purpose of spiritual emergence is to reveal your divine self to you. The most important thing that you need to know is that your past is not the whole story. Think of your past as merely the prologue to the real story of your life. Your real story begins once you awaken and discover who you are and what you are here to do.

Book Two:

Evolution of the Soul

No understanding of evolution is adequate that does not have at its core that we are on a journey toward authentic power, and that authentic empowerment is the goal of our evolutionary process and the purpose of our being.

Gary Zukav

There is much chaos and confusion in societies all over the world. Every day reveals another story of people struggling to survive in a system devoid of soul: rampant disease, mental illness, acts of terrorism, and fearful hysteria are a psychosis of the masses. It appears people are coming unglued at the seams. However, behind the scenes there is a different story to be told. Something magical is happening.

31

For those who are unaware of the mechanics of change, it represents a threat to the familiar comfort zone of safety. Passing from one form, phase, or state to another does not need to be menacing. It is another step on the ladder of life, a necessary transition that creates something better. Change can also be positively viewed as an alteration, new development, modification, reconstruction, or innovation, always with the intention of enhancing and improving, making things better than they once were.

The human race is changing. A mass shift in perception and belief is challenging the old structures and systems in society that no longer function. Consciousness is moving away from the outer-world, physical pursuits of personal survival, sexuality, and power, and moving towards the creative opportunities of inner spiritual love, mystical revelation, unity, and transcendence to find answers. Within the process of this reconstruction, as the world stumbles chaotically through a breakdown, it will become apparent that opposing change will only bring more conflict. Embracing a new awareness and looking at life in a whole new way will reveal the answers. This will require a great leap in consciousness.

Illumination

Understanding how all organisms evolve is key to understanding the current shift in the human psyche. Evolution is a gradual process of transformation from a simple to a complex and better form, unfolding in universal fractal patterns that can be mathematically tracked. These energy patterns follow a system of exponential growth scientists call the Fibonacci Sequence, named after Italian mathematician Leonardo of Pisa, known to us today by his nickname of Fibonacci. This mathematical pattern is a recursive sequence of numbers in which each number equals the sum of the two preceding numbers:

$0+1=1$, $1+1=2$, $1+2=3$, $2+3=5$, $3+5=8$, $5+8=13$, $8+13=21$, $13+21=34$, $21+34=55$, $34+55=89$, $55+89=144$ and on into infinity. [4]

The Fibonacci Sequence represents nature's system of growth. Reaching into ever-higher dimensions, the pattern eternally approaches something unknown, never arriving at an ending. You physically see this fractal system in action as the leaf arrangement on trees, the pattern of florets on

---

4 Mario Livio. *The Golden Ratio.* (Random House Inc., 2002). p.97.

a flower, and the scales on the skin of a pineapple. This energy growth pattern applies to every living thing, from the creation of a single cell, the hexagram configuration of a hive of bees, to growth and population patterns of animals and all mankind. Whatever occurs on a small scale will also eventually be represented on a grander scale reflecting the math of the Fibonacci Sequence.

To better understand the Fibonacci Sequence, it is important to explore the work of Pythagoras. A Greek mathematician and philosopher, Pythagoras (570 – 490 BC), believed that at its deepest level, reality is mathematical in nature and that all numbers are symbols of the universe representing patterns of vibrating energy. He understood the world through the lens of numerical equivalents and through the beautiful order of things beneath the surface of what is seen. His claim to hear the "music of the heavens,"[5] led him to create a system of numerology in which he could explain the metaphysics of numbers that is still used to this day.

The Fibonacci Sequence expands on this divine numerology, dictating cycles of change by the numbers.

---

5 Priya Hemenway. *Divine Proportion.* (Sterling Publishing Co., Inc. 2005). p. 43.

Illumination

As the numerical equation that represents the growth of energy in the physical world, it is also responsible for the unseen structures that bring the physical *into* this world. Consciousness as energy is growing at an astounding rate, along the same proportions as the Fibonacci Sequence. You are also continually being propelled forward, into a literal leap, one in which drastic changes may occur quickly. People all around the world are waking from their slumber and becoming aware of their divine potential in increasingly higher numbers than ever before.

In August of 1987, a most unusual planetary alignment occurred. The Sun, Moon, and six out of eight planets came into a triangular formation known as a grand trine (aligned at the apexes of an equilateral triangle when viewed from Earth). This marked the end of 22 cycles of 52 years each, or 1,144 years in all. The 22 cycles can be divided into 13 heaven cycles beginning in AD 843 and ending in 1519, when the nine hell cycles began, ending 468 years later in 1987. According to historian and new age philosopher Jose Argüelles[6], this rare planetary alignment event came at the end of these "hell" cycles and signaled the beginning of a new age of universal peace, indicating a major energy shift was about to occur. This astrological event was heralded as the turning point in Earth's collective energy, powerful enough to change man's global perspective from one of conflict to one of cooperation.

How does man make such a dramatic leap? Planetary cycles and astrological events are the directives of human consciousness. The archetypal signatures and characteristics represented in each stellar body as it makes its journey closer to the Earth or farther away have an influence on the actions of every living thing within its field of magnetism. Most people are unaware of the effects from these cycles and pay little attention to astrological matters. However, even if many people were unaware of this astrological event, it was clear that people were definitely feeling something.

---

6 Bron Taylor. *Encyclopedia of Religion and Nature.* (London and York: Continuum, 2005). p. 738.

Illumination

Pop culture is a reflection of subliminal patterns in human consciousness. In 1990, a new music recording artist known as "Seal" became famous for his song *"Crazy,"* in which he writes:

> *"But we're never gonna survive unless*
> *We get a little crazy."*[7]

This song's popularity drew attention to the beginning of a wave of change. Something unseen could be felt. Seal described the reaction as craziness and even went as far to suggest that everyone get ready to embrace craziness in order to survive what's on the way.

In 1999 another indicator of change was let loose in the movie *The Matrix.*[8] This avant-garde science fiction film portrayed humans trapped in a form of mental bondage working to free their minds. Although the movie was not fully understood by many, as the countless theory books on the subject matter of the movie will attest, it put an

7 Seal. *"Crazy." Seal.* (Sire Records, 1990).

8 Andrew and Larry Wachowski. *The Matrix.* (Village Roadshow Pictures, 1999).

emphasis on the inner world of the human being and how it is evolving. This awareness became the *tipping point* in human consciousness.

A *tipping point* is a term coined by author Malcolm Gladwell.[9] It describes a moment of critical mass, the threshold or the boiling point, the moment that pushes past the boundaries of normal and into that of change. Essentially, it is an evolutionary leap. Gladwell claims that a *tipping point* has three characteristics[10]:

1. Contagiousness.
2. The fact that little causes can have big effects.
3. Change happens not gradually but at one dramatic moment.

The Matrix had all three characteristics of a *tipping point:*

1. Contagiousness in its attraction of huge audiences all over the world.

---

9 Malcolm Gladwell. *The Tipping Point: How Little Things Can Make a Big Difference.* (Back Bay Books, 2000). p. 12.

10 Malcolm Gladwell. *The Tipping Point: How Little Things Can Make a Big Difference.* (Back Bay Books, 2000). p. 9.

2. The little idea of freeing your mind creating a philosophy with such a big following.

3. The release of the movie and its popularity happening in seemingly one dramatic moment as it played out in cinemas all over the world.

The effects of the trilogy of *The Matrix* movies on the psyche of the masses was incredible. By the end of 2003, after the two sequels *Matrix Reloaded* and *Matrix Revolutions* came into theatres, people deeply questioned both their place in the grand scheme of things and the true mechanics behind how the world functioned. Science fiction, a genre once reserved for the eccentric intellectual, became a mainstream sensation with a new kind of story that stretched the parameters of the mind.

In 2006, sixteen years after Seal was singing his breakout hit, and seven years after the original movie *The Matrix,* a new singing artist known as Gnarls Barkley also came out with a song titled "*Crazy*":

I remember when I lost my mind...

Carrieanne Fonger

…Yeah, I was out of touch

But it wasn't because I didn't know enough

I just knew too much[11]

By the time Gnarls Barkley came out with his hit, the message was changing: "We're all going crazy. I'm going crazy, and it's not all that bad. What is crazy anyway? It's a higher form of awareness."

History is the evolution of thought. The evolving consciousness of the human race allows the world to be seen with new eyes. Everyone reacts to changes within the world and themselves differently. While some people will lash out at society during this process, others will not. Some will use the transformation to move into a new awareness and embrace their divine self. If you could see behind the scenes and into the chemical makeup of these individuals, you would observe that they are currently undergoing the process of divine evolution. According to Charles Darwin and his theory of evolution in the *Origin of Species,[12]* natural selection is ever-present among

11 Gnarls Barkley. "*Crazy.*" *St. Elsewhere.* (Warner Music, 2006).

12 Charles Darwin. *The Origin of Species by Means of Natural Selection.* (John Murray Books, 1859).

all living things, always pushing life forward, tempting it to evolve. Could it be possible that right now, an inner evolution is also taking place?

release from suffering

               and the problem of evil

I find hope in the darkest of days.

His Holiness the 14th Dalai Lama

Opposing forces of nature can never be completely eliminated and are actually necessary for evolution. Good is only good when contrasted with evil, and evil is only evil when contrasted with good. Within the human condition there is a constant struggle to rise above this duality and escape from it.

Evil is created within the ego of man as he unconsciously struggles to survive and serve his "I am" instinctive nature.

When a human being is operating on automatic pilot and reacting to life's situations, the only way to see life is through the lens of separation, of good and evil. From this dualistic point of view, the only way to win is if someone else loses. Illusory attempts to avoid suffering through addictive habits such as drugs, food, sex, shopping, or television, become part of an everyday scenario that supports pleasing the ego. This is the destructive cycle of suffering.

Suffering as the bearing of personal pain and distress is part of the human condition. The never-ending cycle of experiencing hurt and disorder and the trials associated with transcending it is caused by desire. When an individual has a passionate craving, covetousness, or longing for something, the ego's attachment to that desire brings mental, emotional, physical, and/or spiritual pain through the fixed expectation of a certain outcome. Desire becomes a strong motivator and can overpower an individual to the point that a person will do anything to fulfill it.

Mental suffering occurs when an individual is consumed with the mental chatter of the ego and allows it to interfere with reality, assuming that what plays out in the mind is true physically. Emotional suffering is a by-product of mental suffering, in which the beliefs and expectations riddling the mind are so strong that they grow into an emotional charge. These emotions that come with the mental chatter make what is going on inside the mind seem real, often overtaking more sensitive people who allow their emotions to drive their actions. Physical suffering results when the mind is controlled by insistent belief patterns that actually cause a block in the physical body, creating illness. Spiritual suffering manifests when the spiritual seeker allows the ego to run its own agenda.

The ego, that little voice in the head that insists on I and Me, is a feisty little character. Persistently pushy and relentless at times of intense desire, it has a mind and personality all its own. Ego loves to roam in the open spaces of the unconscious states of the mind. The constant desire to feed the ego and its insatiable hunger for "identification and separation"[13] is the foremost cause of suffering.

Suffering occurs when you feel that you no longer have free will. You feel that you have been wronged in some

---

13 Eckhart Tolle. *A New Earth: Awakening to Your Life's Purpose.* (Penguin Group USA, 200). p. 60.

way and your choices have been extinguished, forcing you to make a choice that you would not normally entertain. The greater part of most people's thinking is involuntary, automatic, and repetitive. In this state of mind you are unaware and unmindful of yourself because you are focused on you. When trapped in a state of suffering, you ask, "How can I stop the pain? What about me? Can't you see I'm suffering?"

Attachment to the pain of the past builds up emotional turmoil, and if not checked, creates an addiction in an attempt to ease suffering. Awareness of the feelings behind the desire for affliction is the way out of suffering. Once you are able to become aware of your emotions and understand why you are having them, then it is possible to open a door to transcend the darkness of suffering and bring it to the light.

Buddhism has a system for release from suffering called "The Noble Eightfold Path."[14] Describing the various ways to end personal pain as explained by Siddhartha Gautama (Buddha), it is a practical guideline to ethical and mental

---

14 Theodore Ludwig. *The Sacred Paths of the East.* (Pearson Prentice Hall, 2006). p. 119.

development with the goal of freeing the individual from attachments and delusions caused by the ego. The eight aspects of the path are not to be understood as a sequence of single steps; instead, they are highly interdependent principles that must be seen in relationship with each other.

1. *Right View*

   To see and understand things as they really are, grasp the impermanent and imperfect nature of worldly objects and ideas. To understand the law of karma and karmic conditioning.

2. *Right Intention*

   The commitment to ethical and mental self-improvement.

3. *Right Speech*

   Telling the truth, to speak in a friendly, warm, and gentle manner, and to talk only when necessary.

4. *Right Action*

Act kindly and compassionately, be honest, respect the belongings of others, and keep all relationships harmless to others.

5. *Right Livelihood*

To earn one's living in a righteous way. Accumulation of wealth should be gained legally and peacefully.

6. *Right Effort*

Mental energy is the force behind right effort. The same type of energy that fuels desire, envy, aggression, and violence can also fuel self-discipline, honesty, benevolence, and kindness.

7. *Right Mindfulness*

The mental ability to see things as they are, with clear consciousness.

8. *Right Concentration*

> To focus on wholesome thoughts and actions. Concentration in this context is described as one-pointedness of mind, meaning a state where all mental faculties are unified and directed onto one particular object.

According to Buddhist thought, practicing the virtues of the Noble Eightfold Path will balance the ego, escape from dualistic thinking, and alleviate one's suffering by withdrawing from the acts that create negative karma.

The concept of karma is that of merit transfer,[15] in which all actions, both good and bad, are believed to determine the quality of rebirth in the next life. This cycle continues on for as many lives as needed until there is no more attachment to desire. When the soul releases attachment to suffering, it graduates into an ultimate awakening referred to as Nirvana. With no more karma to work upon, the soul is liberated into freedom.

This is what the Mayans were predicting. During this current cycle, the "Night Before the Dawn," all humans

---

15 Roy C. Amore and Willard G. Oxtoby, *World Religions: Eastern Traditions.* (Oxford University Press, 2010). p.207.

collectively work to transcend their karma, gaining the personal power to evolve beyond it. Transcendence of suffering allows the newly liberated soul to see the world with new eyes.

the magnificence of madness

The greatest blessings granted to mankind come by way of madness, which is a divine gift.

Socrates

During your process of awakening there will come a point when the new life that you are becoming aware of stretches so far past the boundaries of your old, comfortable reality that you will question if you are going crazy. Have no fear, for this is a good sign. It means you are growing in your awareness of self and your place in the world.

This part of the journey is reminiscent of the adolescent phase of your life. You will constantly want to say no, to challenge systems of authority, and to test boundaries. The new awareness of your waking self may be brought into your life in the following three ways:

1. Making a new life decision that breaks away from old patterns.
2. Being pushed and stressed to the brink.
3. Understanding new truths that were not available to you before.

1.) Making a new life decision that breaks away from old patterns:

Your loved ones are used to you reacting to life in the same way that you have in the past. Any change from that behavior challenges their expectations of you and causes them to question how they see you, how you fit into their current system, and judge if you are a threat to their safety. When the defiant action you take seems sudden and not along the old patterns that you have used in the past, people will instantly conclude that something is wrong. You, however, know that nothing is wrong. The light bulb of awareness has doggedly pursued your conscience until you came to the realization that you have to go forward in a different way. Often there is no physical explanation. You just know that you have to do things differently. Don't let anyone talk you out of what you need to do to move forward. The only person that knows what is right for you is you.

2.) Being pushed and stressed to the brink:

You suddenly say no to an insane way of life that you used to think was normal. Living in a constant state of adrenalin rush and fear can only go on for so long before an accident, illness, loss of a job, or any other number of negative situations will make you slow down and question your current state. You constantly wonder if there is another way of doing things, because you know that your current life situation is not working for you. Life doesn't have to be lived this way. Trust your intuition and get out of there!

3.) Understanding new truths that were not available to you before:

There are many lies in your life that need to be uncovered. As you move into a more aware state, you will notice that the lies are in your life because you tell lies to others. The truth is you are lying to yourself. A sudden blast of truth in your life will send the whole foundation crumbling because it didn't have a foundation to stand on in the first place. Stand up and be responsible for yourself! Say NO when you need to, don't make excuses, and take a vow to stick to the truth.

Illumination

No matter what situation puts you out of your mind, it is safe to say that feeling like you are going crazy is exactly where you need to be. It means you are on the brink of a major change. I'm not talking about the straight jacket kind of crazy, but rather an intense throwing up your hands in the air and surrendering to life. Losing control of the mind allows it to open. You begin to not care so deeply for what happens and to allow life to unfold naturally. This letting go also frees you from fear and allows you to begin to embrace out-of-context, nutty ideas that bring nourishment to your soul.

As you begin to get accustomed to the freedom madness brings, you will develop your own special concoction of what works best to feed your soul. A dash of insanity, a dollop of letting go, a pint of hilarity, a shovel-full of courage (or a proper combination thereof), as you mix your personal recipe together. The gift of madness gives you the freedom to entertain anything as a possibility and the courage to put new and amazing ideas to work.

Madness invokes creativity and imagination, inspiring you to ask questions of life such as "What if?" and "I

Carrieanne Fonger

wonder?" It releases you from the shackles of what you know and works under the premise that you know nothing. What a relief. You are now out of the box and the world is your candy store to explore! This soon develops into an insatiable curiosity and desire to learn. Once you have crossed over to this point, you have embraced your insanity and allowed it to show you the way. Congratulations! You have made it through one of life's hardest tests and come out much stronger than you were before.

Madness is a special doorway on the journey. It gives you the freedom to tap into your innate brilliance, and show you what is behind the illusion of the ego.

behind the illusion

You live in a world which is a playground of illusion, full of false paths, false values and false ideals.

Sai Baba

The ability to see the truth is always a matter of perception. When your belief system changes, the world around you will change. When the ego is tamed and no longer controls the unconscious, unaware you, the world will present itself as one connected unit. The now outdated concepts of I and Me will move into a new discovery of We. Obvious moments of synchronicity and coincidence connecting external events continually remind you that there is a higher something happening behind the scenes that is beyond the ego's control.

Recognition of the root cause behind suffering allows movement past the illusion of separateness, ego, and self. This awareness is the point of power, a place where suffering can be transcended through taking responsibility. However, the ego will not give in willingly. It will work its tricks of fear and lies to stay alive.

Fear, an "affliction in the mind due to false projections,"[16] is an instinctual emotion pre-programmed into all living things as a response to a perceived threat or potential danger. When you are living life from the ego and entrenched heavily in a sense of I and Me (ultimately in a state of separateness), everything in your environment becomes a perceived threat. Because the most important thing to a selfish person full of ego is itself, fear becomes a very real part of every moment of every day.

However, to an aware individual who is rid of the negative aspects of ego and has embraced the understanding

---

16 Kate Crosby and Andrew Skilton. *The Bodhicaryavatara.* (Oxford's University Press, 2008). p. 69.

of the connection behind all living things, fear is merely a distraction. The acronym for fear reveals the meaning:

F   False

E   Evidence

A   Appearing

R   Real

Fear is the illusion. It is an untruth, a lie that the mind makes up to try and make logic out of a situation that it cannot understand in an effort to protect the ego.

Fear is also behind what James Redfield calls "control dramas."[17] Childhood traumas create attachment to suffering and therefore block your ability to fully experience life. By creating attachment to suffering, all

---

17 James Redfield. *The Celestine Prophecy.* (Warner Books, 1993). p. 127 – 139.

humans, because of their upbringing, tend toward one of four control dramas:

Intimidators: Steal energy from others by threatening.

Interrogators: Steal energy by judging and questioning.

Aloofness: Attracts attention and energy by playing coy.

Poor Me: Makes others feel guilty and responsible for them.

By becoming aware of your family dynamics that created the personal control drama, you become aware of what types of fear energy are feeding the ego. In this moment of awareness, the fear will reveal itself as an untruth, as an illusion.

At this point it becomes possible to rid yourself of the personal control dramas and expand your personal belief system. Once cleared of personal traumas, you can build energy through contemplation and meditation, and on a new awareness of intuitions, dreams, and synchronistic coincidences, all guiding you in the direction of your own positive transformation.

A conscious, aware person lives beyond a state of fear. After passing beyond the understanding of opposites comes the awareness of the concepts of faith, trust, allowing, and commitment to the truth. By realizing and committing to the truth, fear is replaced by purpose, and that is when you begin to remember who you are.

remembering who you are

Man, know thyself, and thou wilt know the universe and the gods.

Inscription at the Temple of Delphi

The opposite of fear is love. Moving past suffering and illusion, past the scope of separation and into unity consciousness is an expansion of personal awareness and the beginning of a quest to love the self. After your ego has been tamed and stripped away to nothing, it is time to rebuild it in a healthy way. Self-exploration through journaling, spending time in nature, and doing the things you love to do are a crucial step in developing a healthy ego.

Instead of having the ego control you and being caught up in its selfishness, it now takes the place of a positive cheering section, boosting your confidence and supporting you each step of the way as you learn to honour yourself. This form of ego has a self-first attitude, meaning that honouring the self is of the utmost importance in creating a whole person. As an aware individual, you will focus on being the best person you can be in an effort to enhance all aspects of your life. This in turn will radiate outwards and benefit all people around you.

"Know thyself" is a very important part of remembering who you are. Take time to understand your own strengths and weaknesses. Find ways to embrace the weaker parts and work to make them stronger. Discard the parts that you dislike and keep introducing new things to move past that personal comfort zone. Make a special effort to love and accept these aspects of yourself, for they are unique to you. The world of self-first is all about doing what you love and loving what you do to create the foundation for a strong, whole, and healthy person both inside and out. If there is anything in your life that does not fit into this category, then it is time to let it go.

Illumination

Remember, the opposite of love is fear. If you are holding on to things in your life that you do not love, then you are also holding on to fear and holding yourself back.

Getting to know yourself is easy. Approach this exercise just like you would when being introduced to a new friend. What do you like? What do you dislike? What makes you laugh? What makes you cry? Dig deeply and honestly. To reveal the hidden meaning and purpose within, ask yourself these five key questions:[18]

1. *Who am I?*

   This is the question that you need to ask your heart. It is beyond physical description and goes into the soul. Who are you at the very core?

2. *What is important to me?*

   What are the things in life that take precedence? No matter how small or how large, these things nourish the soul and are a key part to examining personal boundaries.

---

18 Carrieanne Fonger. *Enlightenment: One Woman's Journey as an Extrasensory Human.* (Golden Sun Books, 2009). p. 62.

3. *What am I here to do?*

   What are your dreams? What do you love to do? What are your hobbies? What did you want to be when you were a child? What about now?

4. *What are my gifts and talents?*

   Everybody is a genius at something. What are you really good at? What are those natural things that you do so effortlessly?

5. *How can I share my gifts with the world?*

   How can you combine all of the above information and share it with others in a positive way?

Answering these questions truthfully will create the beginning of a commitment to yourself, embracing a higher awareness, one that supports a new kind of personal agenda: *do what you love and love what you do!*

As suffering, fear, and the illusion of separation continue to lose their grip, you will move into a new understanding, one in which you see your true self, your potential, your gifts, and your purpose. The original

Illumination

dreams and goals from childhood will become clear again with new-found enthusiasm. This passion will drive you to make them a reality, and nothing will stop you from achieving your goal.

Book Three:

A New Perspective

rediscovery of the sacred

Luminous beings are we.

Yoda

Every human being has a special purpose. Creating a life based on doing what you love and loving what you do will reveal your purpose to you. Life's work should not be one of toil and strain, but instead should be like your hobby: fun, exciting, and inviting. A purposeful life is something that drives you forward, making you more alive with every thought and action toward it.

This deeper understanding leads to a new form of empowerment: the power to love life in every form that it appears, without judgment and the ability to perceive meaningfulness and purpose in the smallest details of daily living. When you align positive thoughts, emotions, and actions with the highest parts of yourself, you are filled with enthusiasm, purpose, and meaning. Life is rich and nourishing. There are no thoughts of suffering and bitterness. There is no memory of fear. You are joyously and intimately engaged with your world.

The true art of rediscovering the sacred is remembering who you are by paying attention to all those things that you appreciate and have gratitude for in your life.

Recognizing the sacred on the outside allows the sacred within to become visible to the self. This precious awareness can be revealed in the following six ways:

1. *A why to live for, a reason for being.*

Having a reason or purpose in your daily living gives you focus. It creates desires and goals. It ignites fire and passion. In Nietzsche's words, "He who has a why to live for can bear with almost any how."[19]

2. *Love is the answer.*

Love is appreciation. The true art of loving is the art of acceptance. Learning to love everything outside of yourself creates a space for loving the you within.

3. *Nurturing the soul.*

Soul speaks through the small. The path to soul is a collection of life's seemingly small, trivial events that challenge you to respond from your soul. Every time you listen to a friend in need, help a child with homework, or play with your family pet, the soul speaks the loudest. The most important encounters in life are the small

19 Viktor E. Frankl. *Man's Search For Meaning.* (Beacon Press, 2006). p. 76.

moments through which your soul spoke to others, and other souls have spoken to you.

4. *Emptiness: the art of allowing.*

Letting go and allowing life to flow naturally is somewhat of an art. It's not easy to trust that what is happening is for the best. It is in the empty spaces of life that you can reflect and learn.

5. *Meaning, mystery, and myth: exploration of the divine.*

Rediscovery of the sacred is all about the personal exploration of the divine. You have a personal myth to explore and transcend as you begin the walk into your divine footsteps. What does the word *divine* mean to you?

6. *Everything that lives is holy: gratitude, appreciation, and honour.*

The father of Taoism, Lao Tzu is famous for telling people to understand the "ordinary as sacred."[20] Graciousness gives a presence of thankful acceptance in recognition of the abundant world. Honoring yourself with your life's work will reveal the divine plan: *you are here to remember that you are divine.* There is no difference between you and the heavens, the stars, the trees, a babbling brook or the ocean. All things come from the same source. The idea of an authentic and wholesome life is one that is lived in the awareness of the sacred as the center of your world. Every moment of every day, each breath and all things that make up life are honored and respected for the essence of the sacred divine that shines within.

20 Victor, H. Mair. *Tao Te Ching: The Classical Book of Integrity and the Way.* (Bantam Books, 1990).

Soul is such a gentle, delicate aspect of the self. It appreciates subtle nurturing and a constant tender caressing. Personal cultivation and adherence to what is fulfilling is foremost in an individual that tends to the soul. The priority becomes taking the time to understand what the self needs and wants to feel comfortable and at peace in the world.

Tending to the soul is not an event that happens only a few times a year. It is a moment-by-moment event. You must constantly check in with yourself and fill the spaces of the day with meaning, while still finding balance with the necessary actions of the day. It's all a part of a unique give-and-take process.

All aspects of the soul relate to those things in life that are spoken through the small. Daily life is full of little epiphanies encased within the sacredness of the most ordinary things. The most minute details and the most ordinary activities, carried out with mindfulness, have an effect far beyond their apparent insignificance. Mindful pausing, the art of taking time and attending to life without rushing, allows the ordinary to be transcended. When there is time to digest ideas and time to embrace concepts encountered throughout the day, life becomes a source of enrichment. A child's laugh, a dog's wagging tail, a hug, a whisper, or a beautiful flower, are all little expressions of loving appreciation. Each thing is sacred, and therefore within all things there is possibility of nourishment for the soul.

Doing what you love to do, and adopting it as a philosophy to live by, develops a healthy belief system of worthiness. Accessing creativity on a daily basis will allow you to emphasize that which is beyond the ordinary. "When imagination is allowed to move to deep places, the sacred is revealed."[21] Bit by bit, each moment builds on the other. And throughout the course of a day, a week, a year, the collection of sacred experience creates a humble confidence, one that cultivates self-determination and a positive outlook on life.

Exploration through the imagination and dreams become an important tool while on the journey of the soul. Imagination constantly explores future possibilities, while dreams allow the discovery and exploration of certain aspects of the soul that remain hidden during the waking moments of the day. Becoming aware of synchronistic messages, courageous acts, and super physical feats stretch the senses in the realm of what is possible.

---

21 Thomas Moore. *Care of the Soul.* (Harper Collins Books, 1992). p. 289.

mythology of the hero

Wonder Woman:

I'm talking about what we do . . . living a secret life, always in danger every day. It's a never-ending battle. How do you do it?

Superman:

I do it because I have to. People need us. There's a whole world suffering out there. We've been given the power to do something about it. It is our gift . . . the reason we are here . . .

Wonder Woman:
Balance of Power, 2006,
Author Unknown.

Heroes play an important role in the psyche of the human race. In a world where morals and integrity have gone awry, heroes speak for truth and justice. They defend the innocent, punish the guilty, and protect the delicate balance of good and evil necessary for a wholesome way of life. When all else is lost, a hero can save the day. These stories of possibility are popular because everyone can identify with the commonality of these individuals. All heroes were normal people like you and me once, until that fateful day when they discovered their special power within. Da, da, da, da . . .

What is a hero? Whether it's Superman's X-ray vision and the ability to leap tall buildings in a single bound or Wonder Woman's super strength and lasso of truth, all heroes have one thing in common: a solitary journey of the underdog who miraculously receives the power to overcome all struggles with the enhancement of inner power. The evolution of the soul is one and the same journey.

Before comic book heroes, the cultural myth of the hero was traditionally passed along in oral stories. Tales of inspiration and hope have always been an important element within society: some mythical character who can do more than the average person, one who has gone past the normal and into the fantastical realm of the hero and overcomes the obstacles of darkness to achieve the impossible.

The great mythologist Joseph Campbell offers a very interesting theory of the hero's journey.[22] He claims that it is through the story of the hero's journey that humans find meaning and understanding in the importance of their own quest. Campbell's life work focused on uncovering a structure that every hero follows during his path to awareness of purpose. It begins with a *departure* from normal life because of a *call to adventure*, a certain moment when everything is going to change, whether it is welcomed or not (which can be equated with spiritual emergence). This is followed by a *refusal of the call*, where a sense of duty, obligation, fear, insecurity, or a sense of inadequacy works to hold the hero in current circumstances, making

---

22 Joseph Campbell. *The Hero's Journey.* (Joseph Campbell Foundation, 2006).

him or her feel that they can't meet the obligation of their calling.

After an insistent motion to refuse the impending personal task, the hero becomes committed, however reluctantly, to the quest (the evolution of the soul). This triggers action by a supernatural aid, a magical helper in the form of a guide who will reinforce the choice to make a commitment to the journey. Now the hero *crosses the first threshold* into the field of adventure, leaving the known limits of his or her world and into an unknown and dangerous realm where the rules and limits are not known.

The next stage is referred to as the *belly of the whale,* the final separation from the hero's known world and old self. The experiences that will shape the new world and self will begin shortly, or may begin with this experience, which is often symbolized by something dark, unknown, and frightening. By entering this stage, the hero shows willingness to undergo a metamorphosis, to die to him or herself.

An *initiation* has now begun. The first step is the

road of trials, a series of tests, tasks, or ordeals that the hero must undergo to begin the transformation. Often failing one or more of the tests, success is found in the third trial. This reveals a *meeting with the goddess,* when the hero experiences a love that has the significance of an all-powerful, all-encompassing, unconditional love.

As the hero draws nearer to completing the task, there is always an element of temptation. Known as *woman as the temptress,* this seductive element attempts to lure the hero to abandon or stray from the quest. After passing this test, there is the passage of the *atonement with the father,* in which the hero must confront and be initiated by whatever holds the ultimate power in his or her life. This will allow for a complete shedding of the old self. The hero is no longer held at bay by the power of another but is now empowered by self and a feeling of purpose for the journey.

Transcendence through apotheosis is the next step. To apotheosize is to deify. When the hero dies a physical death, or dies to the self, he or she moves beyond the opposites to a state of divine knowledge, love, compassion, and bliss. This is a god-like state; the person is in heaven and beyond all strife. *The ultimate boon* follows as the achievement of the goal of the quest.

Upon completion of the journey, the hero will experience a *refusal of the return*, asking, "Why come back to normal life with all its cares and woes?" The *magic flight* results, when the hero must escape from an impending danger, and the *rescue from without* as the hero's powerful guides assist in bringing him or her back to everyday life.

Returning to normal life brings on the *crossing of the return threshold*, to retain the wisdom gained on the quest, and to integrate that wisdom into a human life. This is extremely difficult because the hero must become a master of the two worlds, achieving a balance between the material and spiritual, both the inner and outer worlds. The resulting endeavor leads to the gift of *freedom to live*, freedom to be true to the self.

Where do you fit into this journey? How far along have you traveled? How far have you yet to go? Joseph Campbell's structure for the journey of the hero is a very important one to examine. The evolution of the soul is a mythical, heroic journey of the human race. It is important to see that you are also on the hero's journey, and there is also a hero within you.

the season of miracles

If you can't be the rock, be the ripple.

Regina Brett

No one knows the how or why of existence. After years of breakthroughs in scientific understanding, the search is still on to find how cells know how to function, how the synapses in the brain know when to fire, and how thoughts come into the mind. How do birds fly in flawless formations at incredible speeds as if powered by one mind? How do the planets know how to follow their course? Are these things miracles? Most would say not. Most people would say that the science behind what makes these things possible is not yet understood.

So what exactly makes a miracle? Is it when a person is dying, pronounced dead, and then comes back to life? What about the healing of a terminal illness, or surviving a terrible car crash without suffering physical effects? Many people might call these miracles. Or perhaps all that is happening is that the science behind it is not understood yet.

The real miracles are everywhere, happening every single day in the background, beneath the existence of all things, like dew drops sparkling on morning spring grass, sunlight dancing in diamond waves upon the ocean, or a strand of pearls attached to the string of a necklace. While not obvious, the ordinary miracles do not want to be, they do not need to be. Their existence is the miracle.

The recognition of all parts of life as a miracle brings awareness that you are also part of the miracle. You have now come to a very crucial point on the hero's journey:

the ability to observe the divine around you, making it possible to observe the divine within yourself.

Astrologically there is an event that occurs every 2,150 years known as the Precession of the Equinoxes. This process entails a slow westward shift of the constellations on a plane of the ecliptic, caused by the precession of the Earth's axis of rotation.[23] The Earth is currently moving through such an event. This new star age, in which the heavens are in the process of shifting from the pole constellation of Pisces to that of Aquarius, is an important event for the evolution of the human psyche.

Alignment of the stars in relation to the Earth activates different modes of awareness in the collective consciousness of man, a change foreshadowed in a popular song from 1969 titled, *"Age of Aquarius/Let the Sunshine In."* This song explains what to expect during the move into the new cosmic Age of Aquarius. It talks of peace,

---

23 Graham Hancock. *Fingerprints of the Gods.* (Doubleday Canada Limited, 1995). p. 241.

love, harmony, and the "mind's true liberation," detailing the re-alignment from the focus on the outer physical world of the Age of Pisces, and moving ever forward into the inner world, the Age of Aquarius.

> *When the moon is in the Seventh House*
> *And Jupiter aligns with Mars*
> *Then peace will guide the planets*
> *And love will steer the stars*[24]

The Sun is another important component in the expanding consciousness of the human psyche. For the first time in approximately 26,000 years, the Sun will rise to conjunct the intersection of the Milky Way Galaxy and the Ecliptic Plane on December 21, 2012. This astrological event aligning the Sun with the Great Central Sun of the Galactic center, activates the heart center of the Milky Way Galaxy, and in turn, all souls within it. "This period can be a time of tremendous transformation if we wake up to our true selves; or, it can be a time of tremendous devastation,

---

24 The Fifth Dimension. "Age of Aquarius / Let the Sunshine In." *The Fantastic Fifth Dimension.* (Soul City Records, 1969).

tragedy, and discontentment if we are unwilling to face ourselves."[25] For, just as Copernicus's discovery of the Sun as the center of the universe some five hundred years ago challenged society with a new way of thinking, so will the discovery of the Central Sun, propelling the human race forward into a leap in consciousness.

The "myth of the eternal return"[26] is a theory created by University of Chicago professor Mircea Eliade, describing the great cosmic ages of man. In his book, he details his findings that throughout all cultures there is a similar story structure of five ages of man. As man moves from a Golden Age, in which life is perfect and serenely pure, each succeeding age is a declination of morals and integrity until he sharply approaches the last age in which he destroys himself. However, have no worry, says Eliade, for the world will not end. Instead, the end of the world is always the signal of a resetting of the grand pattern, a birthing of a new Golden Age in which the cycle will repeat itself again and again.

---

25 Dona Bernadette Vigil. *Mastery of Awareness.* (Bear and Company, 2001). p. 8.

26 Mircea Eliade. *The Myth of the Eternal Return.* (Princeton University Press, 2005).

I have hope for humanity. I have faith in the miraculous process of spiritual emergence and the evolution of the soul, and that as more light shines out into the universe, more light will shine within you and ripple out into the world. If all of life is the miracle, then it is possible. And it begins with you.

Transcend the Darkness.

Move into the Light.

Embrace Awareness.

Evolve beyond Duality into Oneness.

In the Golden Age of Divine Man you begin again.

To the illumined mind the whole world burns and sparkles with light.

Ralph Waldo Emerson

Sources

Amore, Roy C., and Oxtoby, Willard G. *World Religions: Eastern Traditions*. Oxford University Press, 2010.

Barkley, Gnarls. *"Crazy." St. Elsewhere*. Warner Music, 2006.

Campbell, Joseph. *The Hero's Journey*. Joseph Campbell Foundation, 2006.

Crosby, Kate, and Skilton, Andrew. *The Bodhicaryavatara*. Oxford University Press, 2008.

Darwin, Charles. *The Origin of Species By Means of Natural Selection*. London: John Murray Books, 1859.

Eliade, Mircea. *The Myth of the Eternal Return*. Princeton University Press, 2005.

Eliade, Mircea. *The Sacred and the Profane*. Harcourt Inc. 1959.

Fenton, John Y. *Religions of Asia: Third Edition*. St. Martin's Press, 1993.

The Fifth Dimension. "Age of Aquarius/Let the Sunshine In." Soul City Records, 1969.

Fleming, Victor, and Le Roy, Mervin. *The Wizard of Oz*. Metro Goldwin Mayer, 1939.

Fonger, Carrieanne. *Enlightenment: One Woman's Journey as an Extrasensory Human*. Golden Sun Books, 2009.

Frankl, Viktor E. *Man's Search For Meaning*. Beacon Press, 2006.

Frazer, R.M. *The Poems of Hesiod*. University of Oklahoma Press, 1983.

Gardner, James. *The Intelligent Universe*. New Page Books, 2007.

Gladwell, Malcolm. *The Tipping Point: How Little Things Can Make a Big Difference*. Back Bay Books, 2000.

Hancock, Graham. *Fingerprints of the Gods*. Doubleday Canada Ltd., 1995.

Hecht, Richard D. and Smart, Ninian. *Sacred Texts of the World: A Universal Anthology*. The Crossroad Publishing Company, 1962.

Hemenway, Priya. *Divine Proportion In Art, Nature and Science*. Sterling Publishing Co. Inc., 2005.

Livio, Mario. *The Golden Ratio*. Random House Inc., 2002.

Ludwig, Theodore. *The Sacred Paths of the East*. Pearson Prentice Hall, 2006.

Mair, Victor, H. *Tao Te Ching: The Classical Book of Integrity and the Way*. Bantam Books, 1990.

Millman, Dan. *Sacred Journey of the Peaceful Warrior*. HJ Kramer New World Library, 2004.

Moore, Thomas. *Care of the Soul*. Harper Collins Books, 1992.

Osho. *The Spiritual Path: Buddha, Zen, Tao, Tantra*. Ivy Press Ltd. 2007.

Redfield, James. *The Celestine Prophecy*. Warner Books, 1993.

Reed, Henry. *Awakening Your Psychic Powers*. St. Martin's Press, 1988.

Sarvananda. *Buddhist's View: Meaning in Life*. Windhorse Publications, 2009.

Seal. *"Crazy." Seal*. Sire Records, 1990.

Taylor, Bron. *Encyclopedia of Religion and Nature*. London and York: Continuum, 2005.

Tolle, Eckhart. *A New Earth: Awakening to Your Life's Purpose*. Penguin Group USA, 2005.

Vigil, Dona Bernadette. *Mastery of Awareness*. Bear and Company, 2001.

Wachowski, Andy and Larry. *The Matrix*. Village Roadshow Pictures, 1999.

Zukav, Gary. *Seat of the Soul*. Free Press, 1989.

About the Author

Carrieanne Fonger is a Metaphysical Teacher and Spiritual Guide. She assists in bringing consciousness to individuals in pursuit of their best life, showing them how to embrace their gifts, and share their passion, purpose, and meaning with the world.

www.carrieannefonger.com